God's Calling

Searching for your
purpose in life

CHRIS COPPERNOLL

Nashville, Tennessee

The New King James Version (NKJV) ©1979, 1980, 1982, 1992, Thomas Nelson, Inc., Publisher. Used by permission.

Quotations from the New Century Version (NCV) ©1987, 1988, 1991 by Word Publishing, Nashville, Tennessee 37214 are used by permission.

The King James Version of the Bible (KJV).

The Holy Bible, New Living Translation (NLT) © 1996. Used by permission of Tyndale House Publishers, Inc., Wheaton, Ill. All rights reserved.

The New International Version of the Bible (NIV) © 1984 by the International Bible Society. Used by permission of Zondervan Bible Publishers.

The New American Standard Bible (NASB) © 1960, 1962, 1963, 1971, 1972, 1973, 1975, and 1977 by the Lockman Foundation, and are used by permission.

The Message (MSG) © 1993. Used by permission of NavPress Publishing Group.

Scriptures without a specified version listed are paraphrases as spoken by the person interviewed by the author for a Soul 2 Soul broadcast.

J. Countryman® is a trademark of Thomas Nelson, Inc.

Designed by Koechel Peterson & Associates, Minneapolis, Minnesota

Project Editor: Kathy Baker

ISBN: 1-4041-0086-5

Printed and bound in the United States of America

www.jcountryman.com
www.thomasnelson.com

www.s2sradio.com

This book is dedicated to my friend, Mark Sager,

and the graduating class of Leslie High School, 1982.

God's Calling . . .

TABLE OF CONTENTS

God's Calling...
INTRODUCTION

This book was written in the shadows of Rick Warren's instant classic, _The Purpose–Driven Life_, in which he clearly and systematically revealed purpose for the evangelical church and purpose–interested people everywhere. _God's Calling_ is about purpose, too—purpose taught through devout examples of contemporary people who have discovered purpose in the discovery of Jesus Christ. You and I can be inspired by hearing trusted voices telling their own stories of hearing God's Calling. Is a life of faith really so simple as believing, then obeying?

God's Calling us. If you've never trusted Him, try it, and you'll find yourself breaking away from the humdrum, meaningless life. God's Calling us to trust. So come on and answer the call. It's for you.

— CHRIS COPPERNOLL

"THE FATHER IS THE GOAL AND

PURPOSE OF MY LIFE."

—JOHN 14:29 MSG

Chapter 1

LOVE & SERVE
OTHERS

ALWAYS BE HUMBLE,

GENTLE, AND PATIENT,

ACCEPTING EACH OTHER IN LOVE.

—EPHESIANS 4:2 NCV

God's Calling Us to...
BE ONE WHO LOVES

> LOVE IS PATIENT,
> LOVE IS KIND.
> IT DOES NOT ENVY,
> IT DOES NOT BOAST,
> IT IS NOT PROUD.
> IT IS NOT RUDE, IT IS
> NOT SELF–SEEKING, IT
> IS NOT EASILY ANGERED,
> IT KEEPS NO RECORD OF
> WRONGS. LOVE DOES
> NOT DELIGHT IN EVIL
> BUT REJOICES WITH
> THE TRUTH. IT ALWAYS
> PROTECTS, ALWAYS
> TRUSTS, ALWAYS HOPES,
> ALWAYS PERSEVERES.
>
> *1 Corinthians 13:4–8 NIV*

According to Paul, the person who is most Christ–like is not the one who spends the most time in prayer, or who has the best mastery of chapter and verse in the Bible, or who has the most Ph.D's , or who has the most important position of responsibility. No, the one who is most Christ–like is the one who loves the most. That's not my opinion; that's the Word that will judge us in Matthew 25: "Come, you blessed of My Father. Inherit the kingdom prepared for you from the creation of the world" (vs 34). Wow! I'm beloved, blessed, pleasing in the eyes of my heavenly Father to the extent that I have become a beneficiary of the kingdom of heaven. Why? Jesus says, "I was hungry, and you gave me food; thirsty, and you gave me drink; naked, and you clothed me; sick, and you comforted me; in prison, and you came to visit me" (vs. 35, 36).

On that day a lot us are going to protest and say, "Just a moment, Sir. I never saw You in my entire life. I lived out most of my days surrounded by ordinary, dull, uninspired, and uninspiring people. How can You say I was ever kind or unkind to You when I never met You? Then will come the revelation of revelations, the end of the greatest story ever told. Jesus will look into your eyes and mine, and say, "What you did to them, you did to Me. As often as you did it for the least of My brothers and sisters, you did it for Me" (vs. 40).

— BRENNAN MANNING

God's Calling...
FOR ME

An instrument finely tuned is ready to play the world's greatest music. The Christian finely tuned is ready to act on the Lord's greatest commandments: to love God and to love others. Jesus says that when we show love to others, we're loving Him. This is God's Calling, to take our energies and direct them towards others in love.

Calling Out
TO GOD

May I learn to love as Christ loves, learn to care as He does, and put into practice what I have learned.

God's Calling Us to...
LOVE AS HE HAS LOVED US

Love is the very nature of God. In both First John and the Gospel of John, God keeps saying, "You need to love one another in exactly the same way that I have loved you." If we have not grown in our understanding of His love, we will not function in love toward one another. Jesus said, "The distinguishing mark that identifies you as My disciple is the quality of the love you have one for another, not the quality of love you have for an unbelieving world, but the quality of love you have for your fellow disciples." It's astounding to me how people can look at those passages in John 13, 14, 15, 16, and 17; hear what Jesus says about loving one another; and then turn right around and act in an un–Christ–like way. It means either we have never known His love, or we've moved a long way away from our relationship with Him.

— HENRY BLACKABY

God's Calling...
FOR ME

Scripture teaches us to love deeply. To love others in the church, to love our neighbors, even to love our enemies. It's astonishing how we allow this commandment to become discretionary for us. What would happen if we invested the remainder of this day, and then this life, following His commandment to love one another?

Calling Out
TO GOD

Jesus, please place in my heart a deep longing to care for others. Help me to love, not merely as an act of obedience, but because it is my heart's desire.

God's Calling Us to...
LOVE OUR NEIGHBORS

"'LOVE THE LORD YOUR GOD WITH ALL YOUR HEART, ALL YOUR SOUL, ALL YOUR MIND, AND ALL YOUR STRENGTH.' THE SECOND COMMAND IS THIS:'LOVE YOUR NEIGHBOR AS YOU LOVE YOURSELF.' THERE ARE NO COMMANDS MORE IMPORTANT THAN THESE."

Mark 12:30–31 NCV

You need to look at people as ones who bear the image of God, who are profoundly valuable. Your message is not to judge them, to get them to stop smoking, to get the rings out of their ears, or even to get them to stop having affairs. That isn't the message. God is not looking to moralize the world; God is looking to restore the world to Himself, and the result will be morality.

People are so desperately hungry for someone who cares, for someone who's interested. When's the last time you told a story and people listened to you all the way through? I mean, who cares when you tell somebody that you've been to the hospital? Nobody's interested in hearing the details for half an hour. I'm convinced that if we learn to appreciate people and take them seriously, our success in personal evangelism will double.

— LARRY CRABB

God's Calling...
FOR ME

God's Calling us to do that which He does, to care deeply for others. Our world needs almost nothing more than it needs us to genuinely care for one for another. Not everyone will adopt this example, the question is will you or I?

Calling Out
TO GOD

Lord, set a passion in my heart to care for people. Shape my heart into one that cares deeply for others.

God's Calling Us to...
LOVE

Many years ago, I was sitting with June in the living room at home and the phone rang. She picked it up and started talking to someone, and after several minutes I wandered off to another room, as it seemed she was deep in conversation. I came back ten or fifteen minutes later, and she was still completely engrossed.

I was sitting in the kitchen when she finally hung up, a good twenty minutes later. She had a big smile on her face, and she said, "I just had the NICEST conversation!" She started telling me about this other woman's life, her children, that she had just lost her father, where she lived, and on and on . . . I said, "Well, June, who was it?" and she said, "Why, honey, it was a wrong number."

That was June. In her eyes, there were two kinds of people in the world: those she knew and loved, and those she didn't know, and loved. She looked for the best in everyone; it was a way of life for her. If you pointed out that a particular person was perhaps not totally deserving of her love, and might in fact be somewhat of a lout, she would say, "Well, honey, we just have to lift him up." She was forever lifting people up. It took me a long time to understand that what she did when she lifted you up was to mirror the very best parts of you back to yourself. She was like a spiritual detective; she saw into all your dark corners and deep recesses, saw your potential and your possible future and the gifts you didn't even know you possessed, and she "lifted them up" for you to see.

She did it for all of us, daily, continuously. But her great mission and passion were lifting up my dad. If being a wife were a corporation, June would have been the CEO. It was her most treasured role. She began every day by saying, "What can I do for YOU, John?" Her love filled up every room he was in, lightened every path he walked, and her devotion created a sacred, exhilarating place for them to live out their married life. My daddy has lost his dearest companion, his musical counterpart, his soul mate, and best friend.

The relationship between stepmother and children is, by definition, complicated, but June eliminated the confusion by banning the words "stepchild" and "stepmother" from her vocabulary and from ours. When she married my father in 1968, she brought with her two daughters: Carlene and Rosey. My dad brought with him four daughters: Kathy, Cindy, Tara, and me. Together they had a son, John Carter. But June always said, "I have seven children." She was unequivocal about it. I know, in the real–time of the heart, that that is a difficult trick to pull off, but she was unwavering. She held it as an ideal, and it was a matter of great honor to her. When I was a young girl at a difficult time, confused and depressed, with no idea of how my life could unfold, she held a picture for me of my adult self, a vision of joy and power and elegance that I could grow into. She did not give birth to me, but she helped me give birth to my future. Recently, a friend was talking to her about the historical significance of the Carter Family and her remarkable place in the lexicon of American music. He asked her what she thought her legacy would be. She said softly, "Oh, I was just a mother."

June gave us so many gifts, some directly, some by example. She was so kind, so charming, and so funny. She made up crazy words that somehow everyone understood. She carried songs in her body the way other people carry red blood cells—she had thousands of them at her immediate disposal—she could recall to the last detail every word and note, and she shared them spontaneously. She loved a particular shade of blue so much that she named it after herself: "June-blue." She loved flowers and always had them around her. In fact, I don't ever recall seeing her in a room without flowers, not a dressing room, a hotel room, certainly not her home. It seemed as if flowers sprouted wherever she walked. John Carter suggested that the last line of her obituary read, "In lieu of donations, send flowers." We put it in. We thought she would get a kick out of that.

She treasured her friends and fawned over them. She made a great, silly girlfriend who would advise you about men and take you shopping and do comparison tastings of cheesecake. She made a lovely surrogate mother to all the sundry musicians who came to her with their craziness and heartaches. She called them her babies. She loved family and home fiercely. She inspired decades of unwavering loyalty in Peggy and her staff. She never sulked, was never rude, and went out of her way to make you feel at home. She had tremendous dignity and grace. I never heard her use coarse language, or even raise her voice. She treated the cashier at the supermarket with the same friendly respect that she treated the president of the United States. I have many, many cherished images of her. I can see her cooing to her beloved hummingbirds on the terrace at Cinnamon Hill in Jamaica, and those hummingbirds would come, unbelievably, and hang suspended a few inches in front of her face to listen to her sing to them. I can see her lying flat on her back on the floor and laughing as she let her little granddaughters brush her hair out all around her head. I can see her come into the room with her hands held out, a ring on every finger, and say to the girls, "Pick one!" I can see her dancing with her leg out sideways and her fist thrust forward, or cradling her autoharp, or working in her gardens. But the memory I hold most dear is of her, two summers ago on her birthday in Virginia.

Dad had orchestrated a reunion and called it "Grandchildren's Week." The whole week was in honor of June. Every day the grandchildren read tributes to her, and we played songs for her and did crazy things to amuse her. One day, she sent all of us children and grandchildren out on canoes with her Virginia relations steering us down the Holston River. It was a gorgeous, magical day. Some of the more urban members of the family had never even been in a canoe. We drifted for a couple of hours, and as we rounded the last bend in the river to the place where we would dock, there was June, standing on the shore in the little clearing between the trees. She had gone ahead in a car to surprise us and welcome us at the end of the journey. She was wearing one of her big flowered hats and long white skirt, and she was waving her scarf and calling, "Helloooo!" I have never seen her so happy.

So, today, from a bereft husband, seven grieving children, sixteen grand-children and three great–grandchildren, we wave to her from THIS shore, as she drifts out of our lives. What a legacy she leaves; what a mother she was. I know she has gone ahead of us to the far side bank. I have faith that when we all round the last bend in the river, she will be standing there on the shore in her big flowered hat and long white skirt, under a June–blue sky, waving her scarf to greet us.

FROM "TRIBUTE TO JUNE" BY
ROSANNE CASH

Delivered at the June Carter Cash funeral on May 18, 2003,
in Hendersonville, Tennessee.

God's Calling...
FOR ME

> We can draw inspiration from the people around us who live extraordinary lives of love and service, who spark what's best in us. When you hear of Christians exemplifying God's best in their love for others, their service, and in their character, learn their song and sing it.

Calling Out
TO GOD

> Lord, help me leave a legacy of love.

God's Calling Us to...
THE LOVE OF
THE FATHER

I see my son, Christian, almost as a parable. It's as if I'm seeing the unfolding mercy and goodness of God when I look at my child, as if I'm holding thirty-one-and-a-half pounds of the grace of God in my arms every day.

One of the things I say to Christian every night is, "I love your ears, I love your eyes, I love your nose, I love your toes. I love you when you're good, I love you when you're naughty, I love you when you're happy, I love you when you're sad." I don't always approve of everything he does, like when he takes my pale blue suede pumps and flushes them down the toilet, but it doesn't stop me from loving him. I understand the same about God now. There are times when I'll make God happy, and there are times when I'll make God sad, but He never stops loving me.

—SHEILA WALSH

God's Calling...
FOR ME

The most difficult thing for us to do sometimes is accept and rest in God's
love for us. We think the amount of love He has for us is proportional to
who we are and what we've done. Rather, God's love has everything
to do with who He is and what He's done. He has made the first step in
love towards us.

Calling Out
TO GOD

I rest in You. This day bring me peace with You, a fuller knowing of
Your eternal love.

God's Calling Us to...
REACH OUT
TO THE HURTING

I had known for two days I was going to get to see Mother Teresa. She walked out in the humblest of ways, no pretense whatsoever, from one of the humblest of buildings, just cement flooring. It was obvious that she's there for the people. They said, "Mama Teresa, this is Greg Long from the United States. He works with us over at the mission raising awareness and help for the children." She said, "That's fantastic! Do it for the glory of God, Greg. Do it for the glory of God." I'm like, "Hey, yes ma'am." I said, "I just want to tell you what an example you are to myself and everyone in the world of what a Christian should be. Thank you for being an example." She said, "Oh, it's my privilege to do it. For the glory of God and the good of man we do it all."

I left there with a sense of awe and humility, and a kind of a warning to be careful how I treat people. I realized it's all done for the glory of God. If we stacked up all I've done in my life and compared it next to Mother Teresa, it's mountain and molehill, if even that. None of us have the right to get puffy about what we do, because she's done it all and doesn't take anything for it.

The biggest thing to learn from her is that Christ came for the hurting. If I'll reach out to those who are hurting, God will take care of it. Because you know what? Everybody's going to be hurting at one time or another. If we'll just give to the hurting, we'll always have someone to minister to, and God will bring them in at that time as we are showing love to them. That's what I learned from Mother Teresa.

— GREG LONG

God's Calling...
FOR ME

We might not ever serve Christ in India, feeding and healing the poorest of the poor. Still, the needy can be the person sitting across the aisle in a classroom, in the next cubicle at work, or sitting at the dinner table each night. When we identify people in need, that's God Calling our hearts to action. God's children work in their Father's business, serving others in love.

Calling Out
TO GOD

Lord, fill me with Your compassion for people. Open my ears and my eyes to the needs around me. Use me to give Your love to the world.

God's Calling Us to...
BE KINGDOM PEOPLE

> "THY KINGDOM
>
> COME, THY WILL BE
>
> DONE IN EARTH,
>
> AS IT IS IN HEAVEN."
>
> *Matthew 6:10* KJV

When we pray the Lord's Prayer, we pray, "Thy kingdom come, Thy will be done on earth" (Matthew 6:10 KJV). We evangelicals have a tendency to ignore that phrase. We often posit the kingdom of God in another world. But the kingdom of God is something we are supposed to see happen on earth! That's why we must be committed to social justice, to changing the world into the kind of world that God wants it to be, knowing all the while that we can never complete the task. That's what the Second Coming is all about. "The good work that He begins in us," says the Apostle Paul, "He will complete in the day of His coming" (Philippians 1:6).

We are to be a kingdom people working for justice; trying to eliminate poverty; transforming social institutions, like the family, into what they ought to be; and winning people to Christ, which is the most important thing. We do these things with the assurance that the good work that we have begun, what the Holy Spirit has initiated in us, will be brought to fruition, completeness, and fulfillment when the Second Coming of Christ occurs.

—TONY CAMPOLO

God's Calling...
FOR ME

> We feel deeply the clarity of the Gospel when we show love and practical care
> to others in need. For in love all things are made right. His love heals us.
> Our love for others mends their wounds, teaching us all the while why Jesus
> said it is better to give than to receive (Acts 20:35).

Calling Out
TO GOD

> May I remember the poor and marginalized today. Teach me how to show
> mercy and love to others.

OH COME,

LET US SING TO THE LORD!

LET US SHOUT JOYFULLY

TO THE ROCK OF OUR SALVATION!

—PSALM 95:1 NKJV

HE MAKES ME

LIE DOWN IN

GREEN PASTURES,

HE LEADS ME BESIDE

QUIET WATERS

Psalm 23:2 NIV

Every morning I spend an hour alone with Jesus before breakfast, and every afternoon I spend an hour with Him before dinner. I call it "conscientiously wasting time with Jesus." Hanging out with Jesus. Some days I call it "show up and shut up." But all in all, it's kind of a holy loitering. I think it's by our very nature that we spend time with people who we love. Love by its nature seeks communion. So it's not surprising that I would spend time with Paul Sheldon, because he's my friend. That's why I spend time with Jesus. If I'm not meeting Jesus on that level, then it's on a level of duty, obligation, rules, and regulations. Sometimes I may do it; sometimes I may not.

It's a very sound principle of psychology that men move toward what they want. When I wake up in the morning, I don't say to myself, "You should have a cup of coffee." I want it, and I just go make it. If I don't have the desire to pray, I think it's much more honest to say: "Jesus, I really don't want to spend time with You. On my list of priorities, You are not number one. I am too caught up in my busyness, whether it's carving out my career, shaping my ministry, being with friends, or having time for play. I don't desire You above everything else. You are not the want in my life that transcends all other wants. It's very painful for me to admit that, but I know You prefer honesty above anything else. And so tonight, Jesus, I'm going to go to my bedroom. I'm going to lock the door. I'm going to kneel down, and I'm going to cry out to You, the God I half–believe in, for a baptism of fire, to move my 'should' to a 'want', to awaken passion within me, a fierce desire for an intimate, heartfelt relationship with You."

— BRENNAN MANNING

God's Calling...
FOR ME

It's very human to place things at the top of our priority list other than God. This common restructuring of our hearts quickly knocks our lives out of balance. The fast track back happens when we carve out time to spend in the presence of Jesus, reading the Bible and praying. It's wonderful to escape a hectic pace and worship the One who heals and reminds us He is God.

Calling Out
TO GOD

Dear Jesus, make me to lie down in green pastures again. No worries, no fears, no clutter. Only the comfort of Your unmistakable presence.

God's Calling Us to...
INVEST WISELY
OUR TIME

THERE IS A TIME

TO CRY AND A TIME

TO LAUGH.

THERE IS A TIME

TO BE SAD AND

A TIME TO DANCE.

Ecclesiastes 3:4 NCV

Every moment is a gift. Like a present wrapped in colorful paper, we are about to open something of great value, hidden in the moment. We stand on the precipice of doing that which is presented to us in every occasion—utilizing the moment for its best use, seeing the moment become its best gem. The moment is entrusted to us for use. To bury it in the dry sands of our boredom, to tarnish it by the stains of our sin, or to infuse it with the power and love of Christ. To make the moment great.

—CHRIS COPPERNOLL

God's Calling...
FOR ME

Time is money, so they say, a precious commodity. Why not think of the time we're given as a currency to invest in a good stock option? God has given us a great stock tip on where we should invest. He said "store your treasures in heaven where they cannot be destroyed by moths or rust" (Matthew 6:20 NCV). Let's invest our time in eternity, in Christ, and in others.

Calling Out
TO GOD

Father, help me make the most of every opportunity, not to waste time, but to harness and use it for Your glory.

God's Calling Us to...
OPEN GOD'S CUPBOARDS

When I get hungry, I head to our food pantry to see what's inside there to munch on. On the days right before the big shopping day those cupboards can be pretty bare. Sometimes all that stares back is that last can of soup and a jar of sauerkraut. When I come back in thirty minutes, my choices haven't changed.

Sometimes the challenges I face in life send me to the dusty shelves of my mental cupboards to look for solutions, only to find the options there are pretty slim: Stay or go? Take it or leave it? Do or do not? I reheat the choices over and over again, yet as workable solutions, they never become "gourmet." Then I ask, "Why am I searching for answers inside a limited mind, when I can go to my unlimited Father?"

His pantry is like the shelves of a grocery superstore. He's stocked floor to ceiling with possibilities I've never imagined, or never could imagine on my own. Daily crises aren't supposed to be solved with can of soup answers and sauerkraut solutions. Go to the Father.

— CHRIS COPPERNOLL

God's Calling...
FOR ME

God wants us to come to Him for answers to our pressing issues. When we feel there's no solution, it's only our minds that are limited, not His power. Never doubt that our Lord can solve any problem, mend any heart, or fix whatever is broken.

Calling Out
TO GOD

Jesus, I rely on You to help me in my time of need. Lift up my head in times of sorrow. There's nothing You can't handle.

God's Calling Us to...
RELINQUISH, TRUST & SERVE

"OBEY THE LORD YOUR

GOD AND FOLLOW

HIS COMMANDS

AND DECREES THAT

I GIVE YOU TODAY."

Deuteronomy 27:10 NIV

God only gives you grace one day at a time. He doesn't give it to you for a month or for the whole trip. Yesterday is a canceled check, tomorrow is a promissory note, but you've got today to live. You need to get up in the morning and say: "This is my day to serve the Lord. I've got one day, twenty-four hours, to serve Him." You can do anything one day at a time.

I've learned to say, "Whatever, Lord," which has been like a magic phrase for me. No matter what comes into my life, "though He slay me," as Job said, "yet will I trust in Him" (Job 13:15). It's a prayer of relinquishment: "Whatever, Lord. Whatever comes through Your filter, I know Your grace will get me through it."

— BARBARA JOHNSON

God's Calling...
FOR ME

Relinquishing, trusting, and serving God. Is it for His sake, or for ours? We can feel like our service to God is burdensome, when in fact it's for our protection and a refuge for His blessing. Our obedience helps preserve us from the devastating consequences of sin. Like a cargo ship docking in a favorable harbor, God's blessings seem to come more readily to those who obey His commandments in love.

Calling Out
TO GOD

Lord, my part is to obey. Everything else is Yours.

God's Calling Us to...
TRUST HIM FOR OUR TOMORROWS

We never know what twelve months will hold. We never know the joys, we never know the challenges. I don't know if people who are important to me will be handed diagnoses that are not good. I don't know if there will be born another Mother Teresa or another Billy Graham or John Wesley. We just don't know. But what we do know is that a long time ago God knew what the twelve months would hold. He knew the good and the bad and the challenges and the sorrows and the joys, and He won't be surprised by any of it. Whether it's walking over a grassy knoll in a family cemetery or whether it's holding this brand new creature that has your eyes or your jaw line, He won't be surprised by it.

The older I get, the more comforting it is to me. As you get older you realize that there are things that you cannot change. When you're young everything seems possible, and then you get older and a lot of truths settle in. For me, that's when it's been so comforting to say: "He is a lot smarter than I am, He knows me better than I know myself, and He cares so much about the ins and outs of my today, and my tomorrow, and my next week. I have to trust Him for that."

—JANET PASCHAL

God's Calling...
FOR ME

When we try to be God, it only brings frustration. In surrender is peace. Just as children play while adults provide a home, so the Lord cares for His children, not requiring us to "lift" beyond our design, but simply to be recipients of His riches, to obey His instructions, and thrive.

Calling Out
TO GOD

There is peace in knowing "the LORD is good, a stronghold in the day of trouble; and He knows those who trust in Him" (Nahum 1:7 NKJV).

God's Calling Us to...
USE THE GIFTS
HE'S GIVEN

To me it's a real gift to be able to sit down and close my eyes, place my hands on the keyboard, and not know what they're going to go do. They just start doing something that I've never done in my whole life. Suddenly I'm making music right on the spot. Sometimes I think, "I love this, Lord, thank You! You gave me this gift. I pray that I can continue to glorify You with it."

You start messing around and all of a sudden you come across this eight-bar phrase that makes you go, "Wow!" One of those was "Place in this World," one of those was "Friends," one of those was . . . I mean, the list goes on. In all of my favorite songs, the music was written in less than five minutes. It just poured out from the fingertips and there it was. You feel almost guilty for taking credit for it. It's a phenomenon to me and very hard to put into words. I really don't understand how it happens. All I know is it's supernatural and it's the Lord.

— MICHAEL W. SMITH

God's Calling...
FOR ME

You may be a songwriter, teacher, or person with a heart for others, but you are without a doubt gifted. Take hold of your God-given talents and use them in ways that benefit the people around you. God gave you these gifts, and it pleases Him when they are used.

Calling Out
TO GOD

Lord, thank You for the gifts You've given me. Help me how to use them to Your glory.

Chapter 3

SALVATION &
OBEDIENCE

[JESUS] WAS ABLE

TO GIVE ETERNAL SALVATION

TO ALL WHO OBEY HIM.

—Hebrews 5:9 NCV

God's Calling Us to...
BELIEVE AND BE SAVED

This is what the Gospel is: God is not mad at His people, and if other people will go to Him, He will not be mad at them either because of the cross.

We hate that. We want to pay, so off to work we go; it's really important that we not owe. The sign of man's fall is this tendency to be drawn into an "I can earn it" mentality. We have to fight that all the time. If we allow God's Spirit to speak to us, the most dangerous thing we can say is, "Lord, show me myself," because He will do it. I think fallen nature is manifested for the Christian not so much in terms of the sins we commit, but in terms of the purity we commit. The danger is that we can become pharisaical. You've never met a man who wants to be obedient more than I do, and I'm better at it than I used to be. But Jesus didn't die to make me nice; He died to make me His. And out of that flows any obedience that I have.

—STEVE BROWN

God's Calling...
FOR ME

God has already done the work of our salvation. We could never save ourselves, could never get it right or even come close. The good news is we don't have to. Jesus has paid the ultimate, and perfect, sacrifice for all our sins and all the sins of the whole world. We just have to believe.

Calling Out
TO GOD

Help me to rest in Your work on the cross. You have already done what we could never do for ourselves.

God's Calling Us to...
CONSIDER THE CROSS

You know, we glorify this cross to the point that we think it wasn't such a big deal. We talk about it in terms of it being just some little happening. When, in fact, this was the most cruel, the most inhumane way to be put to death. When we begin to think of what that was really like, that those nails were real spikes through real honest–to– goodness flesh. It was real bleeding and torture.

I don't think we know what that's about enough to grasp the concept today, because we really don't understand what God's love is all about yet. The fact is that He really cares for us. I wrote a song called, "I Don't Know Why You Love Me" because that's true in my own life. Songs like "He Loved Me With a Cross" and others are written and recorded because I'm still trying to understand what that was about. How could someone love someone so much that they would go to the cross and die for them? I understand that it should have been me on the cross, my good friends, my wife and kids. But it wasn't. It was Jesus Himself, God in the flesh, and that breaks my heart. I'm still trying to understand that, and I'm certain that I'm not the only one.

I want to sing about the cross. Do you know why? Because it is at that crossroad that people must decide. It is in the light of the cross that mankind must decide which direction to go. It is at that juncture that John 3:16 begins to make any semblance of sense to us. "For God so loved the world that He gave his only begotten Son that whosoever would believe in Him would not perish, but have everlasting life."

—LARNELLE HARRIS

God's Calling...
FOR ME

The cross, where Christ was crucified, tells us about man's sinfulness and about God's love that came to save us. After Christ's suffering on the cross, never again will we, the created, wonder how the Creator feels about us or the lengths He is willing to go in order to save us.

Calling Out
TO GOD

Thank You, Lord, for dying on the cross for me. You did what we couldn't do. Your death tells us just how deeply You love the world.

God's Calling Us to...
GOOD HEALTH

Good health to you! We wish for wonderful health in our mind, body, and soul. A mind that's free from worry, a body strong and vibrant, and a soul at peace. God is interested in every detail of our good health, but especially our spiritual health, because it's our souls He died for. The Great Physician has remedied us with the priceless medicine of His own death, created in the mortar and pestle of the crucifixion of Jesus. By faith in the work of Christ upon the cross we are saved, and nowhere else is salvation found.

— CHRIS COPPERNOLL

God's Calling...
FOR ME

God indeed wants to bless us (Jeremiah 29:11). His blessings come
upon us and accompany us when we obey Him (Deuteronomy 28:2).
Like parents' instructions to their beloved children, His decrees are for
our protection and vitality.

Calling Out
TO GOD

Search me, Lord, and show me how to obey You. I want to live in the
shelter of Your blessing.

God's Calling Us to...
KEEP HIS COMMANDMENTS

A man wrote me a letter and said he'd been having an affair with this woman. He was going to leave his wife and three little girls. A woman was at a hotel waiting for him. He was just leaving a note behind and then slipping away in his car, too much a coward to confront his family. In the car on the way to the hotel to pick up this woman who he was going to leave town with, he heard the song "Love Crucified Arose" playing, and the Lord used that song to convict him. He pulled off the road, and sat there and wept, and got real with the Lord. He turned around, went home, called the motel and told the woman that he wouldn't be coming. He confessed everything to his wife, but I don't think he confessed to his children because they were small children. Months after getting his letter, the family came to one of my concerts, and I got to meet them. Here was this beautiful woman and three beautiful little girls. He was willing at one time to throw them all away.

Having told that story, two others come to mind about a couple of missionaries. Max Lucado was one of them. When Max was still a missionary in South America, he at one point was going to quit. He was going to give up his calling, and then someone gave him a tape—I think it was "Love Crucified Arose" there, too. He heard that song and realized again the calling God placed on his life. We started exchanging letters before he had even written any books. I knew Max as a missionary before I knew him as an author.

I've had a couple of other missionary stories like that where people were going to give up. There was a Chinese missionary, a guy who was on a bus. It was one of those horrible old buses with hard wooden seats that you ride for days just to get anywhere in China. This missionary had left where God had called him to be, sort of like Jonah. Anyway, he had gotten a hold of my record *Poema*, and on his long bus ride when he didn't have anything else to do, he listened to it over and over again. Finally, he turned around and made the twenty-hour trip back the other way. He decided that staying in China was what God called him to do.

— MICHAEL CARD

God's Calling...
FOR ME

We've all been tempted to abandon sense and to do things we feel will satisfy us, but God commands us to obey. Some view God as an all-powerful police officer ready to punish us when we disobey the law. Rather, let's exercise more maturity and see that His commandments are loving instructions intended to protect us (and others) from harm.

Calling Out
TO GOD

Heavenly Father, change my rebellious heart. Grow my obedience like a child growing into adulthood, shedding his immaturity while holding on to his innocence.

God's Calling Us to...
EXCHANGE PRICE TAGS

Shiny bits of metal. Our dreams, so important to us, are like little scraps of plastic and shiny bits of tin foil, and yet we're so reluctant to give them up!

Speaker Ken Davis tells a story about a little girl who buys a bead necklace because it's the most beautiful thing she's seen. She even wears her fake pearls when going to bed. One night while tucking her in, her father asks the girl, "Do you love me?" The little girl says, "Of course, Daddy!" He says, "Then will you give me your necklace?" She won't give him her necklace; it's too precious to hand over. She offers him other toys and possessions, but she won't give up the necklace. Night after night her father asks if she loves him and asks for her treasure until one night he enters her room to find her crying. The little girl holds out her hand and drops her imitation pearl necklace into his. The father smiles, reaches into his pocket, and gives his well-loved daughter a real pearl necklace.

— CHRIS COPPERNOLL

God's Calling...
FOR ME

Porsche or pogo stick? King crab or cold gruel? Which of our dreams are superior to those God dreams for us? Jesus asks us to give up what we mistakenly call precious for what He calls priceless.

Calling Out
TO GOD

Lord, You help me to change all the price tags in my life. What was once unimportant is now the most important. What once led my life, I've left behind me. You're calling me to a greater purpose.

Chapter 4

PRAYER & PERSONAL RELATIONSHIP

"I HAVE HEARD YOUR PRAYER,

AVE SEEN YOUR TEARS; SURELY I WILL HEAL YOU."

—2 KINGS 20:5 NKJV

Someone once asked Mother Teresa, "When you speak to God, when you pray, what do you say?" She answered, "I don't say anything. I listen." So the person said, "Okay, when you pray, what does God say to you?" The answer was, "God doesn't say anything. God listens." Then she added, "If you don't understand that, I can't explain it to you."

I relate to that. That is exactly what my prayer life has become in the morning. I make my requests known to God in the evening, but in the morning I wake up, and I'm just still before God. It's like coming in out of the cold on a rainy night and sitting in front of a glowing fire. You just sit in front of the fire, and the warmth of the fire envelops you and makes you feel so good; it turns you from misery to joy. When I go to prayer, I am just still before God. I let God love me and envelop me and penetrate my being. That experience of prayer makes God very real to me.

—TONY CAMPOLO

> "WHEN YOU PRAY,
> YOU SHOULD GO
> INTO YOUR ROOM
> AND CLOSE THE
> DOOR AND PRAY
> TO YOUR FATHER
> WHO CANNOT BE
> SEEN. YOUR FATHER
> CAN SEE WHAT IS
> DONE IN SECRET,
> AND HE WILL
> REWARD YOU."
>
> *Matthew 6:6 NCV*

God's Calling...
FOR ME

Newcomers to Christ can find it awkward as they begin a prayer relationship with Jesus. They aren't sure what to say, or they mistakenly think their speech needs to be formal. God just wants us to come to Him, speaking like children with the full attention of their loving Father.

Calling Out
TO GOD

Today I will find a quiet place to make time with God, my Father. I will speak to Him with both words and silence, listening for His Spirit and waiting upon His still, soft Voice of response.

God's Calling Us to...
BEGIN A JOURNEY
TO THE SAVIOR

HE HAS PUT

A NEW SONG IN MY

MOUTH—PRAISE TO

OUR GOD; MANY

WILL SEE IT

AND FEAR,

AND WILL TRUST

IN THE LORD.

Psalm 40:3 NKJV

A woman came through a line as I was at a bookstore signing some of my records. She said she had heard me at a totally unrelated event, a Wal-mart convention. I was singing for their sales people, invited in as one of the musicians whose music they sell. It wasn't in a Christian music context at all; I just played my songs and told why I write the songs that I do.

This woman came through and said something had impressed her. She'd never heard me before, but she liked the music, got one of my CDs as a result of that night, and started listening to it in her car back and forth to work. She said she found herself one day just weeping and pulling her car over. She couldn't understand why every time she listened to this music there was this huge hunger and emptiness inside of her. She began to realize, "I don't have what this music is celebrating and talking about." She said, "That began my journey toward coming to realize my need for a relationship with Jesus Christ."

— STEVEN CURTIS CHAPMAN

God's Calling...
FOR ME

How beautiful are the feet of those who bring good news! (Isaiah 52:7) God is calling men and women to Himself, and the invitation may come in a song, maybe even at Wal-mart! By making ourselves available to share, lives will be tuned by the music of the Gospel.

Calling Out
TO GOD

I hear Your voice today, Jesus, calling me to Yourself. My answer: "Yes, Lord!"

God's Calling Us to...
CONFESSION AND FORGIVENESS

People are really good at remembering every little thing we do wrong. Jesus isn't like that. Our heavenly Father isn't like that. Christianity is not to be like that.

I wrote the song "Once in a Lifetime." I like what it says: "No matter where we've been, no matter what we've done, today can be our once in a lifetime." When we ask the Lord Jesus into our heart and we ask God to forgive, He is faithful and just to forgive us. Period! That's it, it's over, it's gone, history, outta here. It didn't happen. It's gone, it's erased.

I wish people could do that. People can't do that, God does that. That's the mighty power of the blood of Jesus—it washes clean completely. "Yesterday is gone, tomorrow may not come. This moment is our once in a lifetime." Right now, you and I, no matter what we've done in our lives, this is mind boggling, we can get down on our knees and say, "Lord Jesus, come into my heart, forgive me of my sins, set me on a new place, let me begin again"—and you can!!! Isn't that unbelievable! Where else can you do that?

When you come before Him with a heart sincerely asking for forgiveness, He will forgive you, and you can start all over again. Your life can begin again, and you don't have to worry about one single thing that happened one moment before. To me, that's what Jesus on the cross is all about, and that is one of the things that excites me about going around and sharing the good news of Jesus Christ. You've got all these people walking around with all this baggage, all these hurts, all this stuff saying: "I'm no good. I'm not good enough to go to church. I'm not good enough to be a Christian. I just can't do this"—and it is a lie of Satan, my friend. You can say, "Jesus Lord, forgive me right now," and He is faithful and just to do so. That's exciting!

— DAVID MEECE

God's Calling...
FOR ME

> God will forgive us for the things we have done. He delights to show mercy! (Micah 7:18) Forgiveness is only a prayer away. We also must learn to forgive others for the wrongs they commit against us, because this is the way of the Kingdom.

Calling Out
TO GOD

> Search me, O Lord, and help bring to my mind the sins I've committed against You and others. Help me to confess each one and to forgive others in my life who have sinned against me. I want to be clean.

God's Calling Us to...
ENTER A HEARTFELT RELATIONSHIP WITH JESUS

Why do I want an intimate, heartfelt relationship with Jesus? It goes back to a night I spent in a cave in the Sargasso Desert in Spain. I was living for months in solitude. I got up every morning at 2 a.m. for what we used to call in the old church "Nocturnal Adoration." I'd go to chapel in the cave and try to spend at least one hour in praise and thanksgiving. On the night of December 13, 1968, during what began as a lonely hour of prayer, I heard, in faith, Jesus Christ say, "For love of you, I left My Father's side, and I came to you—you who ran from Me, who fled from Me, who did not want to hear My name. For you I was covered with spit, punched, beaten, and fixed to the wood of the cross." That was over thirty years ago. This morning, in an hour of quiet time right in this room, I realized those words are still burned on my life.

That night in the cave, there was a crucifix behind the altar. I looked at the crucifix for a long time and figuratively saw the blood streaming from every wound and pore in Christ's body. I heard the cry of His blood: "This isn't a joke. It is not a laughing matter to Me that I have loved You."

The longer I looked, the more I realized that no man or woman could ever love me as He does. I went out in the darkness and shouted into the night, "Jesus are You crazy? Are You out of Your mind to have loved me so much?"

I learned that night what a man had told me the day I went to seminary. I was twenty-three years old. He said, "Kid, you will not understand this now, but on the day you experience the love and the heart of Jesus Christ, nothing else in the world will ever again seem that beautiful or desirable."

— BRENNAN MANNING

God's Calling...
FOR ME

Do you walk and talk with Jesus each day, by faith? Have you ever experienced His esteem for you? There is a Friend who sticks closer than a brother (Proverbs 18:24), who promises to never leave us or forsake us (Deuteronomy 31:6). Jesus calls out to us, "Come and follow," to feel the beauty of His presence and be satisfied.

Calling Out
TO GOD

May I walk with You today, Jesus. You are a Friend to the friendless.

God's Calling Us to...
PRAY

So we fasted and

earnestly prayed

that our God

would take care

of us, and he

heard our prayer.

Ezra 8:23 NLT

Generally speaking, I've found that the Lord answers prayers in ways you're not expecting. He usually answers your prayers a lot later than you think He should, but then it turns out to be just the right answer, time and time again. There have been a lot of times when God didn't answer one of my prayers the way I thought He should, but looking back, I'm really glad He didn't.

There was a girl who I really wanted to marry, but she dumped me. I prayed so hard that the Lord would bring us back together again, but He never did. Then I ended up marrying Barb and being the happiest man I could ever be for the next twenty-seven years. Every once in a while I think about that fervent prayer of mine: "Oh Lord, I want to get back together again with so-and-so." Now, I tell the Lord, "Oh dear Lord, thank You for not listening to me! Thank You for not answering that prayer." Ever since then I've said, "Lord, You're in charge. You make the calls. I trust You." I'm going to let the Lord run things. He knows better about what's going on than I do.

Prayer is largely conversational for me. It's an ongoing, moment-by-moment conversation with the Lord. We talk all day long, especially when I'm writing. I try to make sure I'm in tune with Him. There are those times when I get really down and intense, and I do some real supplication prayer; I'm really crying out to God for an answer or a need or some understanding. But generally, I'm sitting there, or lying on the couch, or awake at night, or walking in the woods, and God and I will just talk, have a conversation. I'll just wonder about things, think about things, jot down little notes, and thank the Lord when He helps me to figure things out.

— FRANK PERETTI

God's Calling...
FOR ME

God answers prayer by granting those things we desire and also by denying our requests. While this is difficult in the short term, His answers are always right and a gift in themselves. We need to seek the Kingdom first, and all the rest will be added to us.

Calling Out
TO GOD

Thank You for unanswered prayers! I know You have only the best at heart for me.

God's Calling Us to...
PRAYER THROUGH
THE HOLY SPIRIT

> WE DO NOT KNOW
>
> HOW TO PRAY AS WE
>
> SHOULD, BUT THE
>
> SPIRIT HIMSELF
>
> INTERCEDES FOR US
>
> WITH GROANINGS
>
> TOO DEEP FOR WORDS.
>
> *Romans 8:26 NASB*

Prayer is absolutely crucial to a Christian's life; it's how we get to know God, how we get to know what is on the heart of God. It's usually in a time of prayer that God makes major adjustments in our lives. Romans 8:26 says that one of our great weaknesses is that we don't know how to pray as we ought, but God has given us the Holy Spirit to help us in that incredible process of prayer. Often when I go to pray, I start in one direction and suddenly realize that my whole heart is moving to pray in another direction. That is the Holy Spirit saying, "Henry, you really didn't know what to pray, but at least you came to pray. Now I'm going to redirect you in your praying so that you will be dead–center in the will of God."

We went through a particularly critical time in our life when we learned that our sixteen–year–old daughter had cancer. I needed to know if there was something that God had in mind in that situation so that I could make the adjustments in my life and then guide our daughter and our family through it. As I prayed, John 11:4 became very real to me: "This sickness is not unto death, but for the glory of God, that the Son of God may be glorified through it."

My whole prayer life changed then to say, "Father, if you are going to be glorified in this, give me wisdom and understanding and counsel and power to go through it and make the right decisions. Help me to always be watching to see how You are going to be honored and glorified through this time." I thanked Him for the assurance He gave me that my daughter's illness was not unto death.

She went through chemotherapy and radiation, and in the middle of it all, the doctors said, "We don't understand it, but we don't see any more cancer." It had been growing in her body for two years! In that situation, prayer and the Scriptures and the Spirit of God had guided us to know what was on the heart of God, how to adjust our lives, and how to be very, very alert to Him.

— HENRY BLACKABY

God's Calling...
FOR ME

In all things we should pray (Philippians 4:6). There never need be a time when we feel our prayers aren't welcomed by God. He is there for us to call out to, so keep praying!

Calling Out
TO GOD

Lord, You love to give direction, wisdom, and answers. You hear us when we pray and care for our concerns.

God's Calling Us to...
REMEMBER
HIS KINDNESS

> "HE IS MY REFUGE
>
> AND MY FORTRESS;
>
> MY GOD, IN HIM
>
> I WILL TRUST."
>
> *Psalm 91:2 NKJV*

Our family has a wonderful little kitty-cat named KiKi that we've raised since she was six weeks old. We love her, feed her, pet her, and let her wander around the house wherever she likes. We let her sleep whenever and wherever she likes, and we let her in and out through the door twenty times a day. But sometimes I wonder, "Why does she still run from us?" You see, she bolts when we come into the room too quickly or reach for her when she isn't expecting it. Does she think we mean her harm after caring for her all her life?

Maybe God wonders the same thing. He's cared for us so long and so lovingly, and yet we still run from Him at times, surprised by His approach, He reaches and we turn away. Since He's given us His kindness, His presence, and His Son, what should we expect His intentions to be?

— CHRIS COPPERNOLL

God's Calling...
FOR ME

God cares for us deeply, and His actions show that. Sometimes the hardest lesson in a believer's life is learning to trust the Father. The good news is that He is wonderfully patient with us, compassionate and gracious, slow to anger, abounding in love (Psalm 103:8).

Calling Out
TO GOD

Lord, help me to trust You more. You are loving and kind; help grow my trust in You.

"… I WILL MAKE THEM CLEAN.

THEN THEY WILL BE MY PEOPLE,

AND I WILL BE THEIR GOD."

—EZEKIEL 37:23 NCV

Healing

Growing

God's Calling Us to...
ASK HIM FOR WISDOM

IF ANY OF YOU

NEEDS WISDOM,

YOU SHOULD ASK

GOD FOR IT. HE IS

GENEROUS AND

ENJOYS GIVING

TO ALL PEOPLE,

SO HE WILL GIVE

YOU WISDOM.

James 1:5 NCV

My favorite promise from God's Word is that if any of us lacks wisdom, we can ask God, and He will gladly give it. The one thing I am convinced of is that I lack wisdom! I don't have a clue. There have been times when a certain thing has seemed great to me, but further down the road I've wondered, "What were you thinking?" Now I think: "Why would you even try to get it right yourself? Why wouldn't you make it a habit to pray in every single situation?" So whether I'm going to a meeting, having a conversation like this one today, whatever I'm doing, I say, "Lord, You know me. I have no wisdom of my own, so I ask right now for Your words and Your wisdom." I pray continuously through the day, whenever I find myself facing situations in which I need His wisdom.

— SHEILA WALSH

God's Calling...
FOR ME

God doesn't intend for us to manage life on our own. He wants us to come to Him for the things we need, including wisdom. Whether it's wisdom for spiritual matters, or wisdom for making decisions in daily living, God is there for us to call on 24/7.

Calling Out
TO GOD

I call on You for wisdom. You generously give to me the wisdom I lack.

God's Calling Us to...
BE CLEANSED, HEALED, AND STRAIGHTENED

O LORD MY GOD,

I CRIED OUT TO

YOU, AND YOU

HEALED ME.

Psalm 30:2 NKJV

A preacher in Los Angeles named E.V. Hill said: "The body of Christ is not made up of clean people, but of dirty people who are being washed clean by the blood of Jesus. It's not made up of well people, but of sick people, and some of us are getting better one day at a time. It's not made up of straight people, but of crooked people who are being straightened out by the Word of God."

And I thought, "That's it; that's us!" We're all dirty and sick and crooked—and by the mercy of Jesus one day at a time we're all trying to get better.

—BONNIE KEEN

God's Calling...
FOR ME

We need Christ's redemption and healing! People are so precious to God that He sent His only Son to die on the cross, and upon our belief in Him, Jesus sets about the work of conforming us to His likeness, Perfect Love.

Calling Out
TO GOD

I am confident in Your work upon the cross, and I embrace the changing in my inner being. Teach me Your wonderful ways!

God's Calling Us to...
COME HOME

> "MY HOUSE SHALL
>
> BE CALLED A HOUSE
>
> OF PRAYER FOR
>
> ALL NATIONS."
>
> *Isaiah 56:7, Mark 11:17*
> *NKJV*

When people share openly about their struggles, the church is being the church. God doesn't work in the darkness. It's a spiritual truth that until things are out in the light, He can't change us. But if we confess our sins, He is faithful and just to forgive our sins. We have to get things out into the light! I believe the church is God's "safe place" to make risky decisions. If the church can be less and less a place where you come to be perfect and more and more a place where you come to be healed, less and less a country club and more and more a hospital, then I think we're heading in the right direction.

I'm under the conviction that for every pain in a given congregation, there is a person in that congregation who can help ease that pain if we can just get those two people together. The problem is, we preachers get in the way. We think we have to fix everything. But it's the Holy Spirit's church, and He'll teach us how to get out of the way.

I like the thought that the church is a home for every heart. Church is a home, a place where people can find protection and safety. Jesus says, "My desire is that My house be a house of prayer for all people; a house where no person is turned away, where the doors are wide open."

It's a home for the heart. The heart is that place where God does the work in the soul of man. Yes, we feed and clothe the bodies of the people we touch, but we're in the heart-changing business most of all.

—MAX LUCADO

God's Calling...
FOR ME

Modern churches work hard to make the seeking, wounded, and restless feel welcomed inside their doors. This is the perfect time to involve ourselves in a church where we can examine what it means to be a Christ-follower within a body of believers. What church has to offer is well worth our getting out of bed on Sunday morning, exchanging our worries for the peace offered only by God.

Calling Out
TO GOD

Jesus, Yours is a house of prayer, worship, and healing. Help me find the good things You have in store for us there.

God's Calling Us to...
HEART SURGERY

EXAMINE ME,

O LORD, AND TRY

ME; TEST MY MIND

AND MY HEART.

Psalm 26:2 NASB

I know God is real because of what He has done in my own interior being. I got to such a place of desperation in my life that I decided I was through with trying all my own ways and knowing all my own answers. I was willing to say, "If You are there and if You care, then do something to rescue me—and I will obey You to the best of my ability." When I got to that place, I began to experience God in many different ways. I could see His handiwork. The Bible says that the heavens declare His glory, and I could see glorious things about God. I could see His fingerprints all over creation. What I needed was to experience those fingerprints inside my own heart.

My husband had to have open–heart surgery because he had blockages behind his heart. The doctors had to saw through his breast bone, pull open the rib cage to expose the chest cavity, reach in, and lift out his heart. They told me, "At one point your husband's heart will be in the hand of a surgeon." And I remember saying, "Oh, he's going to get fingerprints all over it."

That reminds me of our God, how He loves to examine the heart. He's not satisfied with just seeing a mind or an attitude; He wants to look at the very deepest part of the heart. It's as if He lifts it out and examines it. That was what I needed done to me many years ago, and that is what I experienced. It was not easy. There was a breaking, so to speak, as He sawed through and exposed the deepest secrets of my life.

A speaker named Ney Bailey said something once that was so wonderful. It was a question she posed that's used now at the Women of Faith conferences: If there was a video made of your entire life, including everything you've ever thought, everything you've said that you thought no one would ever know about, and it was shown at a local theater to all your family and friends, how would you feel? That's a devastating and frightening thought! Then Ney said, "God has seen your movie, and He loves you." That is what I experienced as He exposed the most frightening parts of my life to the light. I found that I was safe in that examination. He already knew everything there was to know about me, and He still cared passionately for me!

—PATSY CLAIRMONT

God's Calling...
FOR ME

Like a patient on an operating table, we are opened, examined, and changed by the Great Physician. The Master Surgeon knows how to touch and heal the sick, life's battered and wounded. But doesn't the patient need to go to the Doctor first for treatment? When He comes to our door making house calls, can He mend us if we don't let Him in? Open up to God who stands at the door knocking, wanting to come in and heal you.

Calling Out
TO GOD

Lord, I let You in today. Examine my heart. Show me where a change is needed so my heart can beat with love like Yours.

LISTEN CAREFULLY

TO WHAT WISE PEOPLE

SAY; PAY ATTENTION

TO WHAT I AM

TEACHING YOU.

Proverbs 22:17 NCV

I'm thinking of something that happened that was really a life–changing moment for me. It was that point that I think we all come to from time to time when we're going one way and we abruptly go the other way because of an inter-action or an event.

My event was encountering a young boy named Juan. I had received a letter through the mail that this boy wanted to talk with me after a show we were doing. I thought, "His mom went through a lot of trouble to write the letter; I'm definitely going to go." Basically the letter just said that Juan was ill.

Well, I waited before the show to meet them and they never came. I waited during a different segment of time and they didn't come. Then finally at the very last minute as I was walking out of the building someone stopped me and said, "Juan and his mom are here." So I turned around and there was an extraordinary five–year–old boy who was dressed in a three-piece suit. He offered his hand to me, spoke to me like an adult, you know, "Hello, Margaret," and shook my hand. And he had a camera, "Okay, Mom take our picture," and orchestrated the whole thing. He also wanted to take his own picture of me. Juan handed me this bear that he had bought for me along with a note that basically he just dictated and then signed his name.

I was really moved at how mature he was and how incredibly organized he was. I also was very curious about his illness and what would become of him. I took everything he gave me back to my room and immediately opened it up when I got there. I first read the letter from his mom that said basically that Juan had a brain tumor. In all the time he had gone through scans and also chemotherapy and radiation therapy, he had never once had a sedative or a pain killer. The hospital was astounded because this was the only child that they knew of who never took any medication while they underwent treatment. All he would do is take my album *Soul* and listen to it while receiving his therapy. He didn't ever complain, nothing at all like that. The last time the mother took him in, the doctor told her, "Enjoy him, because he won't be coming back." It was his last session and she said he only had a few weeks left.

During those weeks he came to see me. One of the final things he wanted to do was to meet me. I don't know that I have the vocabulary or the artistic integrity to express what that felt like—to know that somebody's last wish was to meet me, someone as insignificant and dismissible as myself. How humbling and then how moving to think that this young life was going to end soon. All that in light of me wishing that I could go back to that moment and make it more of a moment. Me, wishing I that I could do something more, although he didn't request it and he wasn't anxious for it. Yet, it made me stop and assess. I need to pay more attention to these things. I need to be more informed, and I need to realize that these are the moments that count. These are the things that we walk away with. It's not anything else. It's not how many people come to the show or well you sing or don't sing. It's the interaction with people.

— MARGARET BECKER

God's Calling...
FOR ME

What do we value most? Our schedules, our personal comfort, our priorities? Look for the special moments in each day to harvest and use for God's glory.

Calling Out
TO GOD

Lord, help me pay attention to the little things that may be bigger than I realize.

WE KNOW THAT IN EVERYTHING

GOD WORKS FOR THE GOOD OF THOSE WHO

LOVE HIM. THEY ARE THE PEOPLE HE CALLED,

BECAUSE THAT WAS HIS PLAN.

—ROMANS 8:28 NCV

God's Calling Us to...
OVERCOME THE CHARGE OF WORTHLESSNESS

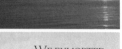

WE EXHORTED, AND COMFORTED, AND CHARGED EVERY ONE OF YOU, AS A FATHER DOES HIS OWN CHILDREN, THAT YOU WOULD WALK WORTHY OF GOD WHO CALLS YOU INTO HIS OWN KINGDOM AND GLORY.

1 Thessalonians 2:11, 12

NKJV

My father passed away in 1986, and I realized after he died a lot of things I'd never faced. My piano was always my life; it's how I communicated with people, it's how I kept going. But my father's alcoholism was something I'd never dealt with. The physical abuse he threw on my mother was something I'd never dealt with. When you're a ten–year–old kid and you watch your dad trying to kill your mother, it does things to you. What happens most the time, and in the case of my brother, my sister, and me, is that we shut down. We didn't want to face those kinds of things; we didn't want to see those kinds of things. It's too painful. My father tried to kill everyone in my family one night. He had a gun and he was rounding everybody up—he was going to kill everybody. We were able to get the gun from him and call the police, and they carried him away. I was maybe 11 years old, and it was the last time I saw my father alive. The last thing he said to me was, "You're worthless."

The impact of that kind of thing can be profound. Most people tell you, "Just forget about it, keep going, you'll do better." Unfortunately, time doesn't always heal. Sometimes the wound is so deep that you really need to go back and face those things and work through them in a realistic fashion using God's Word, prayer, and God's people. That's what the church is for. That's what the Holy Spirit is for. Ultimately, I knew I had to get over this because I had developed over the years—deep, deep inside—a deep hatred for my father for what he did to my mom. I was finally able to forgive him in 1988. The album *Learning to Trust* really summed up the process I went through.

There is light at the end of the tunnel. There is hope. Yes, it's hard and yes, sometimes you fall down and you just don't know if you can get back up again. Sometimes you have the urge to just give up. You might have had all this happen to you when you were just a child. I've talked to people dealing with sexual abuse, physical abuse, and emotional abuse. I've talked to people who are going through battered spousal stages and all this kind of thing. It thrills me to be able to say to them, "Hang in there, it does get better." We'll always struggle, but it will get better.

— DAVID MEECE

God's Calling...
FOR ME

It is not uncommon to be charged with the offense of worthlessness in another's eyes, but Jesus went to the cross for us, and His blood is anything but worthless. Christ's opinion of you and me is the highest regard we can ever be shown, and He has spoken His regard toward us by spilling His very blood.

Calling Out
TO GOD

Your life and death tell me I'm important. Now that I have heard from the Master, what other opinion do I need?

THERE IS ONE BODY

AND ONE SPIRIT,

AND GOD CALLED YOU

TO HAVE ONE HOPE.

—EPHESIANS 4:4 NCV

God's Calling Us to...
THE REPAIR SHOP

A TIME TO TEAR AND

A TIME TO MEND,

A TIME TO BE SILENT

AND A TIME TO SPEAK.

Ecclesiastes 3:7 NIV

When I was a little girl, my aunt gave me an old, very beautiful watch. One night I decided to take it apart to see how it worked. I completely ruined the thing. I couldn't get all the pieces back together, and I was so upset. I finally got the courage to go to my mom and say, "Look, I've ruined this watch." She said, "No, it's probably not ruined, darling. If you have all the parts, we'll take it to a watchmaker."

I would say the same thing about life. So often we feel our life is a mess, and we try to get it all together and tidy it up before we bring ourselves to God. I tell people, don't bother doing that. Bring yourself to the Watchmaker. Bring yourself, with all your broken pieces, to the One who made you in the beginning, because He knows where every piece goes. No matter what your life is like, no matter how awful you think you've been, the one thing I know as deep as the marrow in my bones is that God loves you.

— SHEILA WALSH

God's Calling...
FOR ME

Quality timepieces aren't repaired outside the hands of a skilled watchmaker, nor are we restored properly beyond the tender hands of the Maker of Man. If your life is a jumble of whirling gears, broken springs, and lost parts, go to the One who can take all the pieces and put them back where they belong.

Calling Out
TO GOD

Make me as good as new, Lord. Take each piece of my life and put it lovingly back in its place.

God's Calling Us to...
GROW IN OUR KNOWLEDGE OF THE LORD

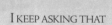

I KEEP ASKING THAT

THE GOD OF OUR

LORD JESUS CHRIST,

THE GLORIOUS FATHER,

MAY GIVE YOU THE

SPIRIT OF WISDOM

AND REVELATION,

SO THAT YOU MAY

KNOW HIM BETTER.

Ephesians 1:17 NIV

The most important thing for all human beings is to know God. I think that's what God wants for us more than anything; for us to know Him more. It's not to create gigantic ministries, it's not to do gigantic concerts, or to become famous, it's to know Him more.

My music, my keyboard, my piano-playing was how I spoke as I expressed myself. But there came a time when God said, "Okay, David, it's time for you to grow. It's time for you to realize that there's much more to life than what you've seen so far." It's a little scary when God says that because life can be very, very difficult. Life can be very, very hard even for the Christian. Sometimes it's even more difficult because a lot of times when Christians really get in touch with themselves, with what's going on around them, and with what God is doing, they hurt even more because they realize just how much they're missing here on this fallen planet.

— DAVID MEECE

God's Calling...
FOR ME

Time spent with good friends is an investment; the dividends come when good friends become old friends. Nothing is more important than our friendship with the Lord. Getting to know Him better enriches everything else in life. Our identity needs to be in Christ, not in how we often view ourselves, whether by race, where we live, or economic status. First and foremost, our identity is found in being His. We are the children of God! He calls us His friends.

Calling Out
TO GOD

Open my eyes, Lord, to see You as a dear friend, the One who calls me by name and clarifies my life with Your perfect ways. When I think of what I value, let me always think of You first, above all else. Amen

Chapter 6

WITNESS

"… YOU ARE MY WITNESSES.

THERE IS NO OTHER GOD BUT ME.

I KNOW OF NO OTHER ROCK;

I AM THE ONLY ONE."

—ISAIAH 44:8 NCV

God's Calling Us to...
EVERY OPPORTUNITY

WHEN WE HAVE

THE OPPORTUNITY

TO HELP ANYONE,

WE SHOULD DO IT.

BUT WE SHOULD

GIVE SPECIAL

ATTENTION TO

THOSE WHO ARE

IN THE FAMILY

OF BELIEVERS.

Galatians 6:10 NCV

When it comes to interacting with people, I think of some of the best things have happened on airplanes. I remember getting on a plane one time and seeing a little girl get on after me who evidently was being flown from one parent to another. She was very sorrowful, her face was exceedingly sad, and she also looked angry. She was probably about eight years old. They sat her next to a mother who had a child with her, and that child was immediately very friendly and warm and tried to draw the little girl into conversation. But the girl would have no part of it. Then the mother tried to talk to the girl, but the girl refused to respond. She didn't want to look at them, much less speak to them. Her lips were tight, her little arms were folded across her chest, and she seemed determined to be miserable.

I began praying for her. I was seated in a way that when she looked up, she was looking right at me. I reached in my purse, found a piece a gum, and began praying that somehow I could communicate without words and break through to this little girl. She looked up at me and I looked at her, and I let a little smile slip across my lips as I lifted up that piece of gum. She looked at me for a moment, then nodded her head to indicate she would receive it. So with her permission, I entered her little circle of reference, gave her that piece of gum, and watched as she totally relaxed and opened up. She began talking with the child next to her, then to the child's mother, all the while looking over and smiling at me. She had had a breakthrough! I really believe it was the Lord's assignment for me that day to pray for that little girl, to help bring her out of a very dark little spot.

I think that many times we deny ourselves an opportunity to be used by God and to be blessed by God because we don't like what we have to walk through. I was blessed by the opportunity to pray for that little girl. I saw God change not only her countenance, but her whole sense of security. It was very sweet to my soul, and it has stayed with me.

— PATSY CLAIRMONT

God's Calling...
FOR ME

> What power we in the Church have, because of His indwelling Spirit, to give out encouragement, interest, and care, just as easily as we would give a stick of gum. The army of God doesn't carry munitions. We're armed to the teeth with His Spirit, ever ready to mend the torn and tattered, knowing that when we give love away it only leaves us richer.

Calling Out
TO GOD

> Thank You for Your care toward the poor and the poor of spirit. May Your example move us into action toward others.

God's Calling Us to...
SHARE OUR FAITH

I PRAY THAT YOU

MAY BE ACTIVE IN

SHARING YOUR

FAITH, SO THAT YOU

WILL HAVE A FULL

UNDERSTANDING OF

EVERY GOOD THING

WE HAVE IN CHRIST.

Philemon 6 NIV

My decision to follow Christ occurred when I was in college. I was a sophomore at Abilene Christian University in Abilene, Texas. One of the things that had held me back from making a commitment to Christ sooner was the old excuse that people who say they're Christians don't always act like it. I figured that when and if I became a Christian, I was going to take it seriously.

I was in Rio DeJanero, Brazil, for five years, from 1983 to 1988. The big challenge was trying to figure out what we in our church had to offer the Brazilians. Though Brazil is primarily Catholic, the real religion there is spiritism, a mystical, very emotional religion. The question we had to wrestle with was this: What do we have to offer them that spiritism does not? We came to the conclusion that we offered forgiveness of sins and victory over death, which is the heart of the Gospel. That clarified for us what our message was. My theology and my message was distilled down to those two things: forgiveness and eternal life.

— MAX LUCADO

God's Calling...
FOR ME

God wants us to be sharers of the faith, sharers of the offer of God's forgiveness and eternal life. He has given so much freely to us, we will be even more blessed when we share our faith with others, and we'll have a full understanding of every good thing we have in Christ.

Calling Out
TO GOD

Lord, bring someone into my life with whom I may share the Gospel. I already anticipate the joy that comes when the love of God grows further into the hearts of men.

God's Calling Us to...
BE WHERE THERE IS FAITH

A man in Dallas came up to me. He had been at the end of his rope and had decided to end it all. He had a bottle of sleeping pills and just swallowed the whole bottle. He was going to turn on his radio to get his mind off of what was about to happen to him. He found a station and had turned it to the Christian station there in Dallas and "Where There is Faith" came on the radio. He said that as he began to listen to the words, he began to weep and realized what he did was wrong. He said he still doesn't know how, but he began to cough up the pills to the point that it wasn't lethal anymore. He found someone who he knew was a Christian, and that person lead him to the Lord that night.

It was neat for him to come and share. He said, "You guys are the reason I'm alive because of what you sang in your music." You can't put a price tag on that. When God uses you in those ways it's incredibly humbling.

—4HIM's ANDY CHRISMAN

God's Calling...
FOR ME

One of the greatest things we will ever experience is seeing a life changed through our telling another about Jesus. Pray for the sensitivity to see others in need, then show His love in word and deed. God has wonderfully saved us from our sins and destruction.

Calling Out
TO GOD

Lord of my salvation, Your Word says I'm your ambassador (2 Corinthians 5:20). What a joy and honor! Help me to see beyond my own needs to the needs of the world, and help me to share with them their need for You.

Chapter 7

STRENGTH TO LIVE

I WILL LOVE YOU,

O LORD, MY STRENGTH.

—PSALM 18:1 NKJV

God's Calling Us to...
CALL ON JESUS

THE CORDS OF DEATH

ENTANGLED ME,

THE ANGUISH OF THE

GRAVE CAME UPON

ME; I WAS OVERCOME

BY TROUBLE AND

SORROW. THEN

I CALLED ON THE

NAME OF THE LORD:

"O LORD, SAVE ME!"

Psalm 116:3–4 NIV

My mom would always teach us, "If you ever get in trouble call on Jesus." I used to think, "Yeah, yeah, alright" until I was walking home from school one day and this man mugged me. He jumped out in front of me, and I looked at him like, "this is not happening!" We lived off a busy street, but every car had stopped—there was nothing. He went to grab at a necklace I had on and grabbed so hard that he knocked me to the ground. Then he straddled on top of me with his legs and bent down. I thought, "Oh my God, I'm about to be raped, killed, and there's no one around!"

I was looking around, "Where'd all the cars go!?" Under my breath I kept saying, "Jesus, Jesus, Jesus." He said, "What'd you say?" and I said, "Jesus?" He was like, "Don't say that!"

I said, "Oh, Jesus!" because I saw this thing worked. I started saying, "the blood of Jesus" remembering my mother say, "Call on the blood of Jesus" so I said, "the blood of Jesus!" and the man got up and ran! He was so mad at me for calling that Name, but he ran.

After that, I went into my house because it had really disturbed me. I thought, "This is deep." I was looking for cars and they weren't coming. I have seven brothers and no one was home. They all could have beat him up, but they weren't there.

So I realized, "Jesus did it. I called His Name and the man ran." The spirit that was leading that man was like, "Don't call that Name!" When I realized that Name was as powerful as it was, I said, "I've got to know who He is."

Ever since that day, I stopped going to church just because I had to. I started going because I wanted to know who in the world He is. Who is Jesus that people could get scared just by hearing His Name? I went to the back of the Bible to find out about Jesus. I looked up the word "Jesus" in the concordance. I got all the things that He did, and then I read the stories about Him. I've just been fascinated with Him ever since because the Name is powerful.

— DEBBIE WINANS

God's Calling...
FOR ME

In times of danger, call upon the Name of the Lord Jesus. The Bible says "from everlasting to everlasting the LORD's love is with those who fear him, and his righteousness with their children's children" (Psalm 103:17 NIV).

Calling Out
TO GOD

Yesterday, today, and forever You are with me. I will trust in Your Holy Name.

God's Calling Us to...
HOPE IN HIS HIGHEST WAYS

THOUGH HE

SLAY ME, YET WILL

I TRUST HIM.

Job 13:15 NKJV

Sometimes our lives are so mundane. Each and every day mimics the day before. Though each day is filled with particulars, when a friend asks, "What's new," you struggle to answer with something fresh. My life was much like that. Though in different areas of marriage, career, and parenthood I had struggles, nothing had touched my life with as many life experiences as the day my daughter went into liver failure and cystic fibroses. Since that day, we have had God literally redefine what a family is about, rediscover our heart motivations and what is important and the things that really don't matter.

After two long years of life–threatening struggle in the hospital, we moved to a new city to be close to Olivia's doctors. The wonderful thing was we were closer to my mom, Olivia's Nana. My husband started a different career, and I became a stay–at–home mom. Financially it was a very hard struggle with the economy so down, but we survived. It was more important to us to be together as a family. Unfortunately, after six months of being in our new city, my mother was diagnosed with a rare lymphoma cancer. The next year has been one long hospital stay for her with very aggressive chemo treatment and three bone marrow transplants. We are still awaiting an outcome for her as she struggles to keep her strength and we surround her with our love to give her support.

Through so many struggles, we have learned that God ultimately has our best in mind. It is very hard to watch your child and your mother struggle to survive, but if you can imagine . . . we have seen so much good through it as well. Our family is so strong! Before, the little things were tearing at the very fabric of our marriage; now it just doesn't matter. We have learned the true meaning of unconditional love. So "though He slay me, yet I will trust Him" means just that. Because every trial, every hurt, every broken heart has the opportunity to give a glimpse of who we are and the chance to hand it over to God and heal.

—BARBARA KING

God's Calling...
FOR ME

> *Life brings with it a lot of difficulty. Can we trust Him when things are*
> *at their lowest? When we are at our weakest? God can do anything He*
> *wants to do with us. But His love for us means a never-ending*
> *Friendship ready to call upon in our darkest hour.*

Calling Out
TO GOD

> *You are Emmanuel, God with us. We cry out and You hear us.*

God's Calling Us to...
PEACE IN A
PEACELESS WORLD

When you go through something that's your worst personal nightmare, when you pray at night that you won't wake up in the morning—I've felt that. I never considered taking my life, but there were times I did not want to wake up in the morning. I remember praying, "God, if there is any mercy left in Your heart for me, please take me home." Since I went through my hospitalization I've had dark moments, but I've never felt hopeless.

We have this bizarre idea that if you love God enough and live a fairly decent life, life will be easy. There's nothing in Scripture to support that. Christ said, "In this world you will have tribulations. But don't worry, because I've overcome what is in this world" (John 16:33). I still have dark days; in fact, yesterday was one of them. I felt sad all day for no particular reason. So I went out to my car, put on some music, and I began to sing to the Lord.

That's what I love about the Psalms of David. They were not supposed to be something we read for five minutes at night, then we close the book and go to bed. Those were the songs of the church that the people sang together, and they sang them out loud. They sang out their pain, and they sang out their joy, and that's what I do, too. That's what I encourage people to do who struggle as I have with depression. Get your Bible, open to Psalms, and pray them out loud. Pray them on days when tears are rolling down your face, and pray them on the days when you are laughing.

—SHEILA WALSH

God's Calling...
FOR ME

One of God's greatest gifts is peace, the stillness of the soul resting in His Presence. Our confidence is that He is complete and is completely in charge. In the quiet of prayer, in the reading of the Scriptures, He meets with us and gives us His peace.

Calling Out
TO GOD

Thank You for overcoming the world. My confidence in You is sure because of who You are.

God's Calling Us to...
PERSEVERANCE

WE ALSO REJOICE

IN OUR SUFFERINGS,

BECAUSE WE KNOW

THAT SUFFERING

PRODUCES

PERSEVERANCE;

PERSEVERANCE,

CHARACTER; AND

CHARACTER, HOPE.

AND HOPE DOES NOT

DISAPPOINT US,

BECAUSE GOD HAS

POURED OUT HIS LOVE

INTO OUR HEARTS BY

THE HOLY SPIRIT, WHOM

HE HAS GIVEN US.

Romans 5:3–5 NIV

I read a quote by Eleanor Roosevelt in which she said, "You must do the things you are afraid of, because it's only in facing your fears that you will ever be free." I've found that to be absolutely true in my own life. If you had asked me as a teenager to name my greatest fear, I would have said, "That I would end up like my dad." He ended up in a psychiatric hospital when he was thirty–four. Well, I ended up in a psychiatric hospital when I was thirty–five or thirty–six. It is one of the greatest things to face your greatest fears. When you walk through them, stumbling at times, you come out with bloody knees, but you come out on the other side with a greater understanding not only of the grace and love of God, but of the fact that He can take you through anything.

After I got out of the psychiatric hospital, I met with a counselor, a very godly man, three times a week for three years. One of the most profound things he said to me was, "Sheila, Jesus has not come to get you through this; He's come to live in you through this." That's why, when I stand up in front of fifteen thousand women on any given weekend, I know that what I say from that platform is true: "God will sustain you, whether you've just been diagnosed with breast cancer, or your husband just left you for another woman, or your child did not come home from the hospital." I understand Romans chapter five more than I ever did before: "Therefore, we rejoice in our sufferings, because suffering produces perseverance; perseverance, character; and character, hope; and hope does not disappoint us."

—SHEILA WALSH

God's Calling...
FOR ME

Phobias and fears can debilitate us from the freedom of life that God intends. Jesus' presence has the power to tear down the strongholds of fear we face. No matter what we struggle with, God is greater and He is mighty to save.

Calling Out
TO GOD

When I am afraid, I know You're there. You are my protector, my sanctuary, and my peace. Nothing is greater than You.

God's Calling Us to...
STAY IN THE GAME

If you are involved in a legalistic church, you can reduce everything to formulas. You can reduce everything to nice little packaged teachings. If someone comes into your office and says, "My marriage is hurting," you can say, "Go to this family life conference, read this book, do this, do that, obey, take three in the morning, and call me next month." If your paradigm of spirituality is simply rules and obedience, things don't get that messy. But if you know the Gospel, you realize that the Father is not simply rearranging deck furniture on the *Titanic*. He's changing our hearts, and that makes you get far more involved in people's hearts and lives.

There have been times when I've felt like quitting. There have been times when I've felt like I used to feel back when I told God I'd never be a pastor. I've thought, "Lord, I'm overwhelmed. It's too much!" But truly, the longer I am alive and the more I understand the Gospel, the more short-lived those seasons are. It has been said that the church is like Noah's ark; if it weren't for the storm outside, you couldn't stand the stink inside! Life in the body of Christ is very messy, and until we're glorified there is going to be pettiness, failure, and people bailing. There's going to be longing, confusion, fear, and pain.

At times I think I'd rather do something else other than pastoring. Maybe Ed McMahon will show up, or I'll win the lottery. I'll move to Montana, fly fish, and write books. Those moments are profound, they are powerful, and they are real. But the Gospel brings me back to my sanity, and I say, "Lord, I'm not my own. You call me to live wisely. You call me to pace myself. You know what You're doing, and I trust You."

— SCOTTY SMITH

God's Calling...
FOR ME

Each of us can become worn by the friction of two conflicting worlds, Earth and Heaven, one churning above, the other below, with us stuck in between. God intends for us both to rest and to remain faithful to the Calling He's placed on us. The apostle Paul said the struggles we face in this world are nothing compared to what we will experience in Heaven.

Calling Out
TO GOD

Lord, help me put into perspective the petty frustrations in this life, especially when seen against the backdrop of Your glory.

God's Calling Us to...
TRUST HIM WHEN LIFE'S TOUGH

"AND THE LORD,

HE IS THE ONE

WHO GOES BEFORE

YOU. HE WILL BE

WITH YOU, HE WILL

NOT LEAVE YOU NOR

FORSAKE YOU;

DO NOT FEAR

NOR BE DISMAYED."

Deuteronomy 31:8 NKJV

We've been through some tough, tough times in our family. My wife almost died, and my daughter had cancer. I had a son who decided not to walk closely with the Lord. We've had times when finances were scarce. I've been in the middle of things that were way beyond me. But I've never found myself discouraged in the sense that most people use the term. I've always felt it would be very difficult to stand in the presence of a Holy God who is everything He says He is, look into His face, know what He's like, and be discouraged.

All the way through the Bible, the people God chose were put into situations that were way beyond themselves. For instance, Moses with Pharaoh. But Moses knew that once he heard from God, it didn't matter what Pharaoh said or how Pharaoh threatened. Pharaoh could not cancel what God had said. I look at Abraham, who went out with just a handful of men and a few allies to defeat the kings who had just defeated five other kings. But Abraham knew God would bring the victory, so he didn't get discouraged. When Daniel was thrown into the lion's den, he didn't get discouraged because he knew God.

One biblical hero who was broken over what he knew from God was Jeremiah. His heart cried out because he knew that God was about to destroy His own people. He knew that if they didn't turn back to God, judgment would come, and it would be thorough. That broke Jeremiah's heart. I don't think he was discouraged in the sense that he thought the situation was hopeless. He did want to get out of the assignment, but he couldn't because God's Word burned in him. He couldn't *not* do the will of God.

I've been in many, many situations where I've faced opposition. I didn't know what was coming next. I didn't know the future of some things. But it never crossed my mind to leave the ministry. I always thought of those moments as my greatest opportunities to experience God. I always said: "Lord, put me in the most difficult, impossible situation, because whatever happens next, it will have to be You. I want to know You, and if I can handle it on my own, I probably won't be calling on You. But if I can't handle it, You're going to have to intervene, and then I'll come to a great experience with You."

I stay in the Scriptures and the Spirit of God, knowing that I'm going to encounter those tough times. God already has put in place the truths about Himself that are going to be important for me to know and to adjust to when those times come. When I hit those discouraging moments, I know that God has already gotten everything in place that I need to face those moments. Though I've never faced them before, they're not a surprise to God. If I can keep my faith and trust in Him and not look at circumstances, then I can go through any situation.

—HENRY BLACKABY

God's Calling...
FOR ME

It's easy to lose heart when our problems seem insurmountable, but one of life's great lessons is learning that nothing is impossible to God. In fact, when we face confusion and crisis in life, they can be God's opportunity for us to recognize our own limitations and His own limitlessness. In any circumstance, He is able to turn situations around. Nothing is impossible to God.

Calling Out
TO GOD

Whether the day is sunny and bright, or cold and rainy, I know You are with me. No matter what confronts me, You are there.

MAY HE GRANT

YOU ACCORDING TO YOUR

HEART'S DESIRE, AND FULFILL

ALL YOUR PURPOSE.

—PSALM 20:4 NKJV

Chapter 8

PEACE WITH GOD

PEACE HAS COME

THROUGH JESUS CHRIST.

JESUS IS THE LORD OF ALL PEOPLE!

—ACTS 10:36 NCV

God's Calling Us to...
DISCOVER GRACE

> HE IS SO RICH
>
> IN KINDNESS THAT
>
> HE PURCHASED OUR
>
> FREEDOM THROUGH
>
> THE BLOOD OF HIS
>
> SON, AND OUR SINS
>
> ARE FORGIVEN.
>
> *Ephesians 1:7 NLT*

The end of the book of Malachi is followed by four hundred years of silence. Then God chooses to show up in the most glorious, unprecedented way, and it's not to the people you would imagine He would show up to. It's not to the impressive people in town, the people you want to hang with, or the people who can get things done. God shows up to the night shift, to the boys on the hill.

When I tell this story to women in conferences, I say: "You're so used to hearing the story of the messenger of God appearing to shepherds on the hillside that you forget how outrageous that is. So let me put it in a different context. Imagine that it is one minute to midnight. Stella and her cleaning crew at the local hospital are getting ready to put out their cigarettes, fill their buckets with hot, soapy water, and mop the corridors. Their hearts and minds are full of worries. Stella is worried about her husband because he is drinking again. Another woman is worried because she's sure her teenage daughter is sleeping with her boyfriend. Each of the women faces private struggles that seem bigger than themselves.

"Suddenly a loud noise comes from the end of the corridor. It seems to be emanating from the operating room, which should be empty at this time of night. They grab their mops (insufficient weapons if something bad were really happening!), hurry to the end of the hallway, and open the door. There stands the most glorious sight Stella has ever seen in her long, hard life. With a wingspan of a thousand eagles, a messenger from God says, "Stella, to you is born this day a Savior, who is Christ the Lord. To you, with your PMS and your varicose veins and your bag full of worries, to you is born a Savior!"

I think this is the most radical way that God could have shown up, not to the religious leaders of the time, not to someone sitting on a throne, but to ordinary men and women carrying with them the burdens of life. And saying to these ordinary people, "To you is born a Savior."

The word "Savior" doesn't only mean someone who is going to rescue us; it means someone who is going to save us and heal us. We're saved in that moment we first respond to God, but then we begin a process that continues for the rest of our lives of being slowly healed by the love of God.

—SHEILA WALSH

God's Calling...
FOR ME

Can anything on Earth be compared to God's love? The awe–inspiring story of Christ's arrival, told in a new and different setting, hearkens our hearts back to the wonder of God's design for the redemption of the world. He cares about the "ragamuffins" in life, and He cares about you.

Calling Out
TO GOD

Lord, we're in awe of what You're doing! Take our excitement and passion and mold it into something useful that serves Your purposes and the people of the world.

God's Calling Us to...
TRUST IN HIS POWER

Six months ago I went to speak at a church. An hour of worship preceded my two-hour lecture that night, and at about a quarter till eight, I found myself praying. I was going to be speaking in fifteen minutes, but I was caught up in the worship. I said, "Lord, if this "connecting" stuff that I'm teaching about is from You, I just have to know it. You've got to let me know. If I've simply made it up because I have a fertile mind and now that I'm getting older I want something new to talk about, let me know so I can dump the whole thing. But if this is a message from You, I want to know it."

This is what I was praying silently to myself in the front row of the church. Then I said, "Lord, I'd love to know Your answer this weekend." That last line was just one of those weird little prayers that popped out of my heart and through my mouth. Within a few minutes of praying that prayer, some guy I'd never met before came up to the front row, stood next to me, and said, "Can I have a word with you?" My thought was, "This is a bad time. I'm going to be speaking in ten minutes to a thousand people, and I've been sitting here praying and worshiping and getting ready, and I don't want to talk to you

LORD, ANSWER ME

BECAUSE YOUR LOVE

IS SO GOOD.

BECAUSE OF YOUR

GREAT KINDNESS,

TURN TO ME.

Psalm 69:16 NCV

right now." But I'm more polite than that! I said, "Sure, what do you want?" He said, "I'm one of the pastors here, and ever since I knew you were coming to our church, I've been praying for you every day. I believe God wants me to say something to you." Well, I'm not used to hearing that kind of thing, but he continued, "I sense that you're struggling with whether your message is from God or not. You really want to know, and you want to know this weekend. I'm here to tell you that you're going to know this weekend." I thought, "What is going on here!?!"

That's the sort of stuff that ten years ago I would have debunked and called silly. But I don't believe it's silly. I've been confining the Spirit far too long. That was an experience that led me to say: "Lord, there's something so real about You. Yet You're so confusing to me. Why couldn't You be real on schedule? Why couldn't You be real in the ways that I've prayed for that have gone unanswered? Why do You come through at a moment like this?"

God is so unpredictable, so unmanageable, so untamable! But every now and then, He does something that makes me say, "You're really there, and my life is in Your hands!"

— LARRY CRABB

God's Calling...
FOR ME

> God is a rekindler of faith. He comes often in our times of weakness, using
> our doubts as a platform to build up our faith. God is ready with a huge
> "Yes!" whenever we ask Him to grow us, to show us more of who He is.

Calling Out
TO GOD

> Father, grow my faith in You. Thank You for entering my uncertainty and
> creating for me an ever–increasing garment of faith.

God's Calling Us to...
HUMILITY

AND WHAT DOES

THE LORD

REQUIRE OF YOU

BUT TO DO JUSTLY,

TO LOVE MERCY,

AND TO WALK

HUMBLY WITH

YOUR GOD?

Micah 6:8 NKJV

I am sitting next to my oldest daughter, Kellye, in the hospital room. She broke her arm last night and is waiting to have surgery. As she sleeps soundly, I'm amazed at her trust in the staff and her doctor, knowing the pain that lies ahead because she's broken this arm before.

I'm currently unemployed. At 46, I'm one of those people who don't know want they want to be when they grow up. God's blessed me with gifts, talents, and abilities, but I've never sensed that He's called me to a particular career. Why am I here, Lord? What is my purpose? What do You require of me?

Growing up, my dad had one job. In twenty-one years I've had seven. At 26, God was in a box. Leaving college, I dreamed that I'd go to work for one company. There'd be a white picket fence around my home, healthy children, two cars in the garage, weekends fishing with the guys, and a healthy retirement. Talk about being naïve! At 46 I have more questions than answers, and He's out of the box. The formulas don't work for me, and the times have changed. I'm reminded of the Scripture "consider it pure joy when you face trials of many kinds" (James 1:2). Often I want to surrender to doubt, fear, and self-pity; then I ask God a question: What do You want from me? And He speaks to me softly through His Word: "Love me, Don. Love mercy, and come humble yourself and walk with Me because I love you. Just as Kellye is trusting in these doctors, trust and abandon yourself to Me."

Could it be that our purpose in life is to spread God's love to others and to let others love us with the Gospel of God's grace? I had an agenda today; God had a different one. He wanted me to brush my daughter's hair from her forehead.

—Don Moss

God's Calling...
FOR ME

Greatness in the Kingdom of God looks very different than it does here on earth. Our Father is pleased with our trust in Him, the abandoning of ourselves to His plans over our own. Life brings with it so many changes, yet God never changes, nor does His love change.

Calling Out
TO GOD

Dear Lord, thank You for caring for us. Grant us many years. Though we may change over the duration, Your love and compassion never fail, never diminish, never cease.

God's Calling Us to...
RENEWAL

HE SAVED US BECAUSE

OF HIS MERCY.

IT WAS NOT BECAUSE

OF GOOD DEEDS

WE DID TO BE

RIGHT WITH HIM.

HE SAVED US

THROUGH THE

WASHING THAT

MADE US NEW

PEOPLE THROUGH

THE HOLY SPIRIT.

Titus 3:5 NCV

I've had images of God that were grounded not in the God who is, but in the God of my experience, the God of my culture, the God of people I grew up with.

The real God needed to cut through all of that. He has confronted me in my fears, my brokenness, my longings, my foolish mistakes, and He has dismantled many wrong images I had of Him. I used to think of Him as an indifferent, distant Father. I used to think of Him as a cosmic killjoy who wanted to find out what I liked to do just so He could say, "No." He needed to dismantle those images, and He lovingly did.

—SCOTTY SMITH

God's Calling...
FOR ME

Do you hold incorrect images of who God is? Have pictures embedded in your mind developed a faulty idea of the Father? Our God is a revealer, and He has revealed Himself in Scripture. Through His Holy Spirit and the Word, He wants to reveal Himself to you.

Calling Out
TO GOD

I want to seek You once again. Help me find You in the Word and rediscover the One who pursues my heart.

God's Calling Us to...
REST IN HIS LOVE

LONG AGO THE LORD

SAID TO ISRAEL:

"I HAVE LOVED YOU,

MY PEOPLE, WITH AN

EVERLASTING LOVE.

WITH UNFAILING

LOVE I HAVE DRAWN

YOU TO MYSELF."

Jeremiah 31:3 NLT

You can either see God as a loving God or as a judgmental and harsh God. If God is a judgmental and harsh God, we wouldn't be here. We have not met up to His standards; we have fallen too many times. I think the very fact that I still have breath tells me that God is a loving God, because He has kept me around this long.

If I can accept the fact that God is a loving God, then I can look at the kind of love that He is. His love is not the kind of love we have on earth; it's a divine love. It's a kind of love that doesn't increase if I'm better or decrease if I'm worse. It's a remarkable kind of love that says, "I'm going to love you independently of what you do." My actions have a thermostatic impact on other people's love for me. If I said bad words to you right now, your love for me would diminish; if I said nice words to you, your love might increase. I can impact and control to a certain degree the amount of love people have for me. Not so with God's love. I cannot change His love. I cannot make it more or make it less.

I think that's the most fascinating truth of Scripture and the one thing I wish people understood about God. We frequently have people walk into our building who don't feel loved. I try to tell them, "It's not up to you to decide if you're loved; that's God's decision, and He said, 'I love you with an everlasting love.'"

—MAX LUCADO

God's Calling...
FOR ME

God's love isn't hypothetical; it's the backbone and the foundation of our relationship with Him. Some things are completely settled, and God's love for His creation is one of those things. So let us not again wonder, "Does He love us?" Rather, let us proclaim, "He loves me, for the Bible tells me so."

Calling Out
TO GOD

Dearest Lord, Your love for me is the most exciting and wondrous thing I know. When I get down I can always remember that Your love for me is eternal, and You are with me always, even to the end of the age.

CONCLUSION

" …FOR THIS PURPOSE

I HAVE RAISED YOU UP,

THAT I MAY SHOW

MY POWER IN YOU,

AND THAT MY NAME

MAY BE DECLARED

IN ALL THE EARTH."

Exodus 9:16 NKJV

Let me tell you a short story . . .

There once was a small, rocky island lost in a vast sea, far from the coast of the closest mainland. For centuries, the people of the small island toiled in the rock-ribbed hillsides to grow enough food. It was far from a tropical paradise—wars frequently broke out as the island people struggled over territory, power, and possessions.

But sometimes at night the island forefathers told fantastic stories of a world on the other side of the sea. That world was plentiful, they said. Food wasn't planted on stony hillsides, but in fertile green fields. There a man could walk for days and never feel confined. The people liked to dream that such a place existed, but they didn't believe such a place could really be.

One day a boy wondered if the stories the old men told could be true, so he built a boat to cross the mysterious sea, risking his life to find the land they'd spoke of, but that no one had ever seen.

After many adventures, the rugged boy washed ashore in the New World, where he was greeted by family and given a royal welcome. The New World was lush and beautiful, everything the island fathers had described, only much more. It was limitless and wonderful.

Live in His Strength

When I think about the challenges in the world, I feel ...

... strong / weak / empowered / helpless / brave / frightened / hopeful / hopeless.

I believe God specifically helped me when:

I feel like God let me down when:

In considering the challenges in the world, I believe God is calling me to rely on Him more by:

Peace with God

I trust God. *Yes / No*

I believe I can live in true peace on earth. *Yes / No*

I understand that peace often comes through pain. *Yes / No*

I believe God loves me—totally, unconditionally, eternally. *Yes / No*

I find peace in the circumstances of my life. *Yes / No*

I find peace in the Giver of my life. *Yes / No*

I want to know more about God's peace. *Yes / No*

In considering the failures of human peace, I believe God is calling me to share His peace by:

God's Calling...

ACKNOWLEDGEMENTS

Grateful acknowledgement is made to W Publishing Group and Howard Publishing for permission to reprint some content from the following books.

Coppernoll, Christopher 1998.
Soul2Soul: Top Christian Artists Share an Intimate Look at Their Lives, Their Music, & Their Faith.
Nashville, Tennessee: Word Publishing

Coppernoll, Christopher, 2001.
Secrets of a Faith Well Lived: Intimate Conversations with Modern Day Disciples.
West Monroe, Louisiana: Howard Publishing Company

The author also wishes to thank Don Moss, Barbara King, and Rosanne Cash for permission to include their stories in this book.

For More Information

Founded by Chris Coppernoll in 1994, *Soul2Soul Radio International* has promoted the Gospel of Jesus Christ as expressed by contemporary Christian artists through their music and honest interviews. Heard in over 500 radio outlets around the globe, *Soul2Soul* provides music and content free of charge to radio stations, missionaries and broadcasters across the United States and in Europe, the Far East, Australia, and South America. *Soul2Soul* is a non-profit organization that takes seriously the call to present a contemporary view of the life of faith in Christ to people everywhere.

www.s2sradio.com

Soul2Soul Radio International
P.O. Box 2543
Brentwood, TN 37024

God's
Calling